Contents

DAILY LIFE
Read here to learn what life was like for the children in these stories, and the impact that migrating had at home and at school.

NUMBER CRUNCHING
Find out the details about migration and the numbers of people involved.

Migrants' lives
Read these boxes to find out what happened to the children in this book when they grew up.

HELPING HAND
Find out how people and organizations have helped children to migrate.

On the scene
Read eyewitness accounts of migration in the migrants' own words.

Some words are printed in bold, **like this**. You can find out what they mean by looking in the glossary on page 30.

A country of immigrants

The United States is a country of **immigrants**. Everyone who lives there has family who once lived in another country. Even the American Indians may have come from another land. Some scientists believe they crossed into North America through what is now Alaska more than 10,000 years ago.

"The streets are paved with gold"

Between 1815 and 1914, more than 30 million people **migrated** to the United States. Some, like the Chinese, went to work on the railways and in the mines. Irish and Jewish immigrants went because of troubles at home. All of them went to America looking for a new life. People had heard the streets were paved with gold. They came to get their share.

More than 100 million Americans have family members who came to the United States through the immigration station on Ellis Island in New York.

On the scene

A poem displayed in the Statue of Liberty has these words:

Give me your tired, your poor

*Your huddled masses **yearning** to breathe free*

Many immigrants to America were poor people looking for a better life. They could identify with these words.

For many immigrants, the Statue of Liberty in New York was the first view of their new home.

Scotland 1849

Immigration to the United States exploded in the middle of the 1800s. By the 1850s, 2.6 million people a year were going to America. Most of these people were from the United Kingdom, Germany, and Scandinavia. Many were drawn to America by the rich farmland of the **Midwest**.

Nature boy

John Muir was born in Dunbar, on the south-east coast of Scotland, in 1838. He fell in love with nature when he was only three. His grandfather took him on walks in the country, and showed him the fruit and wildlife. He had a small plot to tend in the family garden.

One night in 1849, John's father came in with exciting news. The family was moving to America. John would go on ahead with his father, his older sister, and his younger brother. His mother would stay behind with the younger children until the family was settled.

DAILY LIFE

John Muir and his friends played in the ruins of Dunbar Castle, which was close to where he lived. It was more than one thousand years old. There would be no castles for him in his new home.

John Muir grew up in this house in Scotland.

To the New World

It took six weeks to cross the ocean by ship. John's father and sister stayed below with the "old folk", but John and his brother went on deck. They watched the sailors, and played with other boys.

The ship carried many **emigrants** (people who were moving from their original country) to North America. John's father had planned to settle in Canada, but when he heard about the fine soil in the state of Wisconsin, he made that their destination. Wisconsin had just become part of the United States the year before.

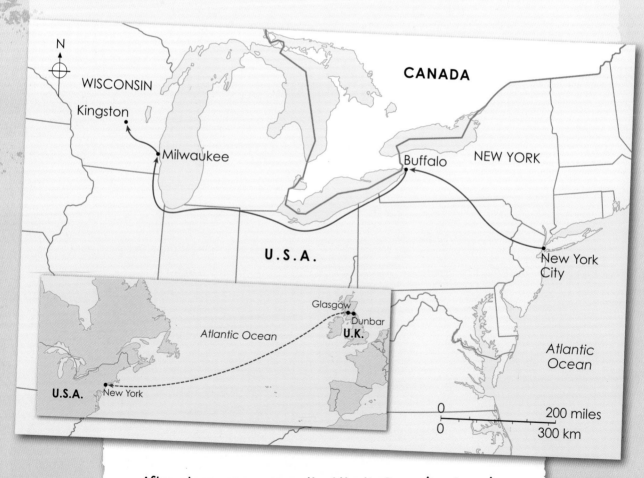

After a long voyage across the Atlantic Ocean (inset map), John Muir and his family travelled more than 1,600 kilometres (1,000 miles) to the middle of Wisconsin (main map).

John Muir loved to draw. When he was a boy, he sketched this picture of his home in Wisconsin.

Hard work

As the oldest boy, John was expected to help build the family home and plough the fields. It was hard work for a boy of eleven. John's father was strict. He made sure his boys completed their work.

John still found time to wander in the woods and fields near his home. He was delighted by all the new birds and other wildlife he discovered.

Learning from the frogs

John spent hours discovering the wildlife in the lake near his home. He studied the birds and fish, and the snakes, bees, and water bugs, too. When his father gave them some wood, John and his brothers quickly built a boat.

John wanted to learn to swim. His father told him, "Go to the frogs, and they will give you all the lessons you need." By watching the frogs, the boys learned how to dive and surface, and how to use their arms and legs.

John Muir's ideas led the US government to create the national park system. These giant redwood sequoia trees are in woods named after him in the state of California.

The long walk

When he grew up, John worked in a factory. One day, a tool cut his eye. The accident nearly left him completely blind. When he recovered, he knew he had to follow his own path through life. He walked from Indiana to Florida (from the northern United States to the south) in just under two months. The walk covered 1,600 kilometres (1,000 miles). He later made his home in California.

Yosemite National Park, in California, is known for its glaciers, waterfalls, and beautiful valleys.

John Muir

John Muir's love of nature never left him. As an adult, he played a part in **preserving**, or saving, many beautiful places. He pushed to create Yosemite National Park, and helped **found** the Sierra Club. This organization still works to preserve the environment today.

China: 1880

In 1849 Chinese immigrants started going to California for the same reason many other people did: gold. Some went to look for the gold. Others set up shops to sell goods to the gold miners.

The farmer's son

Lee Chew was born in China in 1864. When he was 10 years old, he went to work on his father's farm. In China people did not live on their farms. Instead, they lived together in a village.

Lee Chew grew up in a small farming village like this one.

When Lee was 16, a man returned from America to the village. The man had left the village as a poor boy, but he came back rich. He had made his money as a merchant (someone who buys and sells things) in a place called New York City. The rich man built a huge house and gave a great **feast**. Seeing this man filled Lee's head with thoughts of making his fortune in America.

The men of Lee Chew's village worked on farms. They grew many crops, including rice, beans, and sugar cane.

DAILY LIFE

Lee Chew grew up in a small house with his parents, his grandfather, his older brother and his wife, and their two children. How many people do you live with? Would you like to live with so many different members of your family?

To America!

Lee begged his parents to let him go to America, and finally his father gave his blessing. He gave Lee $100 (about £65). Lee travelled to Hong Kong with five other boys from his village. There, he bought a **steerage** ticket on a ship sailing east. Steerage was the cheapest ticket.

Many immigrants came to America in steerage. The journey was uncomfortable, but the tickets were cheap.

The trip was both exciting and confusing for Lee. His grandfather had told him stories about the American wizards and their evil ways. Now Lee was afraid to eat their food. Finally, the ship landed in San Francisco. Lee found a place to live in the Chinese part of the city. There he could get a decent meal.

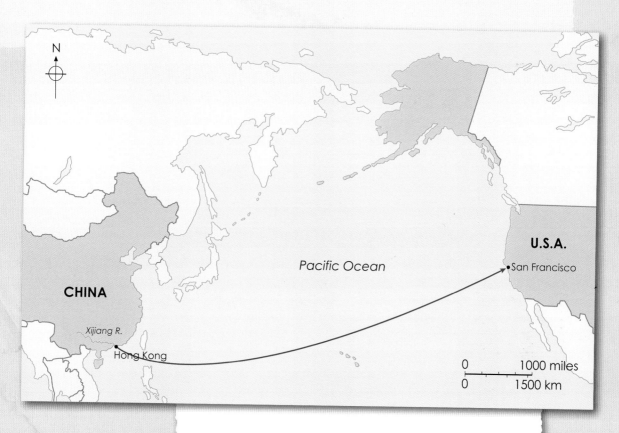

Lee Chew travelled nearly 11,500 kilometres (7,000 miles) from Hong Kong to San Francisco.

NUMBER CRUNCHING

In 1880 there were more than 100,000 Chinese men living in the United States, but fewer than 5,000 Chinese women. Like Lee Chew, many young men came to America on their own, and sent money home to their families.

Working for a living

A man in the Chinese **quarter**, or neighbourhood, got Lee a job working as a servant. He couldn't speak English, and didn't know anything about housework. The mother of the family he worked for showed Lee how to cook and clean. Lee got along well with the family. He was paid $3.50 a week. That's about $75 (£50) today.

Many Chinese people were forced to live in separate neighbourhoods from white people.

After around two years as a servant, Lee had saved $400 (£250). He opened a **laundry**, which is a business that washes clothes. Many Chinese people owned laundries because other jobs were not open to them. Lee later wrote that there are no laundries in China. Everything he knew about cleaning clothes, he learned in America.

Lee eventually moved to New York, where he opened a shop. Years later, he wrote about his experiences in America.

Some Chinese people ran shops like this one.

HELPING HAND

Many white people felt that the Chinese were taking their jobs. In 1882 Chinese people were no longer allowed into the country. Today other groups have trouble immigrating to America. The National Council of La Raza and the Central American Resource Center helps Mexican immigrants with legal, work, and rights issues.

17

Ireland: 1892

In 1892 a new immigration station opened. It was on Ellis Island in New York. Before that time, immigration was managed by individual states. In 1890 the **federal government** took control of immigration. The first person through the gates of the new station was an Irish girl named Annie Moore.

From Ireland to New York City

Annie grew up in Queenstown, Ireland. When she was 14 years old, she set off for the United States with her two younger brothers. Their parents had gone to the US four years earlier. This wasn't unusual. Parents often went ahead to find work and a place to live. When they had enough money, they would send for the rest of the family.

Annie and her brothers set sail from Queenstown, Ireland on 20 December 1891. This town is now called Cobh.

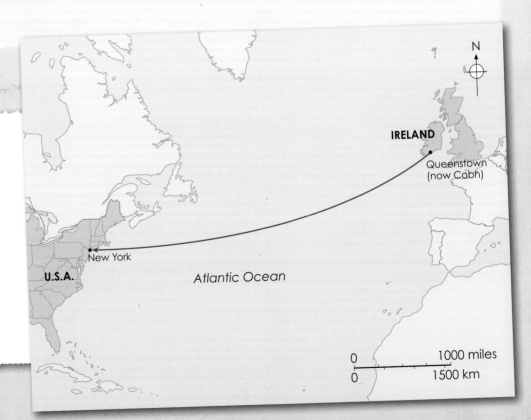

Annie, Anthony, and Philip left Ireland on 20 December 1891. They landed 12 days later, on New Year's Eve.

The immigration station at Ellis Island is now a museum and historic site.

NUMBER CRUNCHING

Between 1892 and 1954, 12 million immigrants passed through Ellis Island. More than one million of them were children.

On Ellis Island

Annie and her brothers were **processed** the next day. That means workers filled out the papers to allow them into the country. According to newspaper reports, another passenger let Annie and her brothers pass in front of the crowd, saying, "Ladies first!" In honour of being the first passenger registered, Annie was given a 10 dollar gold coin.

Life in the city

Life in New York City was hard. Annie and her family lived in a **tenement**, which was like a block of flats that housed many poor people. Annie's father was a **longshoreman**, a man who works loading and unloading boats. The family never had much money.

Tenement buildings housed many poor families.

First immigrant

Annie is still remembered as the first immigrant at Ellis Island. She is a symbol of the dreams of all the immigrants who came to America.

This statue celebrates Annie's arrival at Ellis Island.

Annie Moore

When Annie grew up, she married a baker and had children of her own. Like many immigrants, she worked to give her children a better life than the one she had.

HELPING HAND

The Ellis Island Foundation helps people trace their history. Visitors to their website can search for family members who came to America.

Italy: 1894

In the mid-1800s, most immigrants came from northern European countries, such as Germany and Norway. By the end of the century, more Jewish, Greek, and Italian people were coming to America. They often had a difficult life.

Garibaldi LaPolla was born in 1888 in a small town in southern Italy. When he was still very young, his father left Italy for the United States. He was not alone. More people from Italy have migrated to the United States than from any other country.

This is what Garibaldi's home town of Rapolla looks like today.

In 1894, when Garibaldi was six years old, his father sent for the rest of the family. They journeyed across the ocean to New York. Once in America, they took a train to Montreal, in Canada. This is where Garibaldi's father was living.

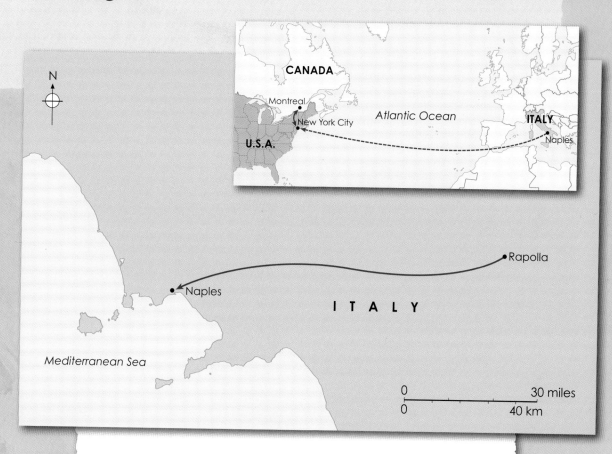

Garibaldi's family went from Rapolla to Naples (main map). From there they sailed to New York City and then travelled north to meet Garibaldi's father (inset map).

DAILY LIFE

Young Garibaldi LaPolla learned to love food and cooking from his father. He would help out at the bakery and watch his father in the kitchen. Many years later, he wrote a cookbook. It was called *Italian Cooking in the American Kitchen*.

Return to New York

Soon the Garibaldi family moved again. They returned to New York City in the United States, where they lived in East Harlem. This area was settled by the Dutch, and was once an expensive neighbourhood. By the 1890s, it was home to African Americans and poor immigrants.

East Harlem was home to many poor people, both black and white.

HELPING HAND

In the late 1800s, settlement houses began to open across the United States. These organizations offered food, clothing, and education to poor people. Union Settlement opened in East Harlem in 1895. It continues to operate today.

Garibaldi went to **public school**. There he learned English, and fell in love with the language. Soon he was making up his own stories.

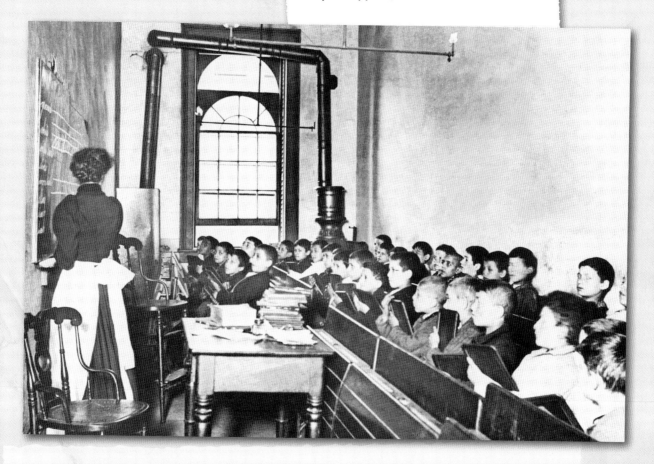

Public schools in Garibaldi's day looked like this.

Telling his story

Garibaldi grew up to be a teacher and writer. In 1935 he wrote a novel called *The Grand Gennaro*. This was a book about growing up in East Harlem, based on his childhood experiences. For many people, this book was their first view of the struggles of Italian immigrants in America.

The melting pot

Some people called the United States a "melting pot". They saw it as a place where people from many different countries come together. The immigrants leave their old ways behind and become Americans.

A salad

In recent years, people have starting seeing the United States as a salad instead. All of the parts come together as something new. Each part still has its own flavour. Instead of leaving their cultures behind, new immigrants add them to the American culture.

People from around the world bring new customs and ideas to the United States.

Immigration today

Immigration to the United States continues today. Each year, children go there from Eastern Europe, Asia, the Middle East, Mexico, and Central America. They will help create the United States of tomorrow.

NUMBER CRUNCHING

Immigration to the United States boomed during the 1800s and early 1900s. In the years between 1820 and 1920, nearly 10 million immigrants arrived from Germany and Ireland alone.

Country	Total
Germany	5,500,000
Ireland	4,400,000
Italy	4,190,000
Austria-Hungary	3,700,000
Russia	3,250,000
England	2,500,000
Sweden	1,000,000
Norway	730,000
Scotland	570,000
France	530,000

This chart shows the number of people who went to the United States from 10 different countries between 1820 and 1920.

Mapping migration

During the 1900s, people went to the United States from many different countries. As you can see on this map, most people went into the country in New York. Lee Chew, like many Asians, entered in San Francisco.

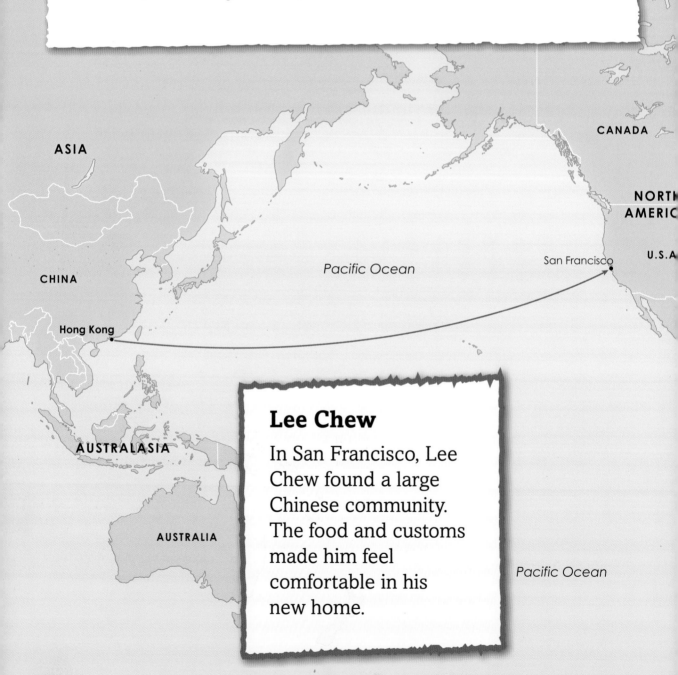

ASIA

CANADA

NORTH AMERICA

CHINA

Hong Kong

Pacific Ocean

San Francisco

U.S.A

AUSTRALASIA

AUSTRALIA

Lee Chew

In San Francisco, Lee Chew found a large Chinese community. The food and customs made him feel comfortable in his new home.

Pacific Ocean

Arctic Ocean

John Muir

John Muir was excited to leave home on a new adventure. In America, he found many natural wonders to delight him.

Annie Moore

It took nearly two weeks for Annie Moore to cross the Atlantic Ocean with her two brothers. They landed in America on New Year's Eve.

SCOTLAND
• Dunbar

IRELAND
• Queenstown

EUROPE

Montreal
gston •
ITALY
• Rapolla
New York

Garibaldi LaPolla

As with many immigrant families, Garibaldi LaPolla's father went to America first, to find work and send money home. The rest of the family followed later.

Atlantic Ocean

SOUTH AMERICA

AFRICA

Indian Ocean

Glossary

emigrant person who leaves their country to live in another one

feast large meal, usually for a special occasion

federal government government of a whole country. The federal government of the United States is based in Washington DC.

found create an organization. John Muir founded the Sierra Club.

immigrant person who used to live in another country

laundry business that washes clothes. Some hotels send their sheets and towels to laundries to be cleaned.

longshoreman person who loads and unloads ships

Midwest central part of the United States. The states of Illinois, Iowa, and Indiana are all in the Midwest.

migrate leave one's home to live somewhere else

preserve keep something from being destroyed. John Muir wanted to preserve the natural beauty of the United States.

processed cleared for immigration. At Ellis Island, processing sometimes included a medical exam.

public school in the United States, a school funded by the government (what is called a state school in the United Kingdom). Children do not need to pay to go to public schools.

quarter neighbourhood where one kind of people live

steerage cheapest kind of travel on a ship. Steerage passengers travel at the bottom of the boat.

tenement crowded block of flats, usually in a poor neighbourhood. Tenements were often very run down.

yearn want something badly. You may yearn for a new bicycle for Christmas.

Find out more

Books

Changing Cultural Landscapes: How Are People and Their Communities Affected by Migration and Settlement? (Investigating Human Migration & Settlement), Marina Cohen (Crabtree, 2010)

Moving People: Migration and Settlement (Geography Focus), Louise Spilsbury (Raintree, 2007).

Websites

tenement.org/foreal
This is a webcomic about the experiences of three recent immigrants to the United States.

www.ellisisland.org
This site includes information about the history of Ellis Island. It is also possible to do a search for passengers on ships that landed there.

www.bbc.co.uk/northernireland/schools
Go to the A–Z section of the "Quick links" menu on the left and find "Tandy". Click on "Famine" to use interactive resources to explore the story of the Great Famine which caused many Irish people to emigrate to America.

www.unionsettlement.org/history
At the bottom of this page there is a video showing a brief history of the Union Settlement Association.

Place to visit

Merseyside Maritime Museum
Albert Dock
Liverpool
L3 4AQ
Telephone: 0151 478 4499
Visit the Emigration gallery to learn more about the million people who sailed from Liverpool between 1830 and 1930 in search of a new and better life.

Index